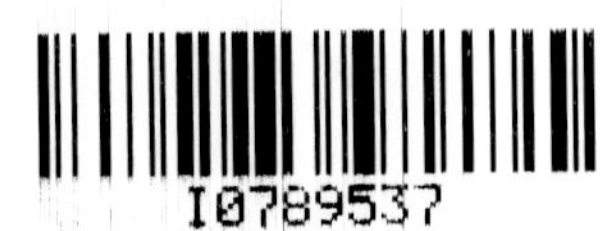

Coloring book for adults and kids amazing dove image for design

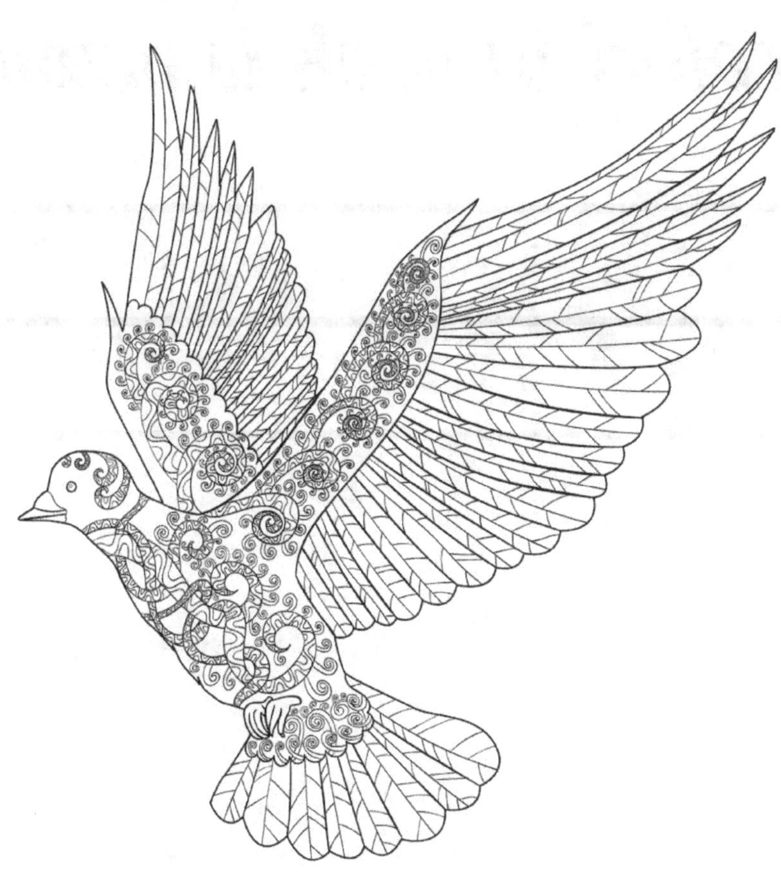

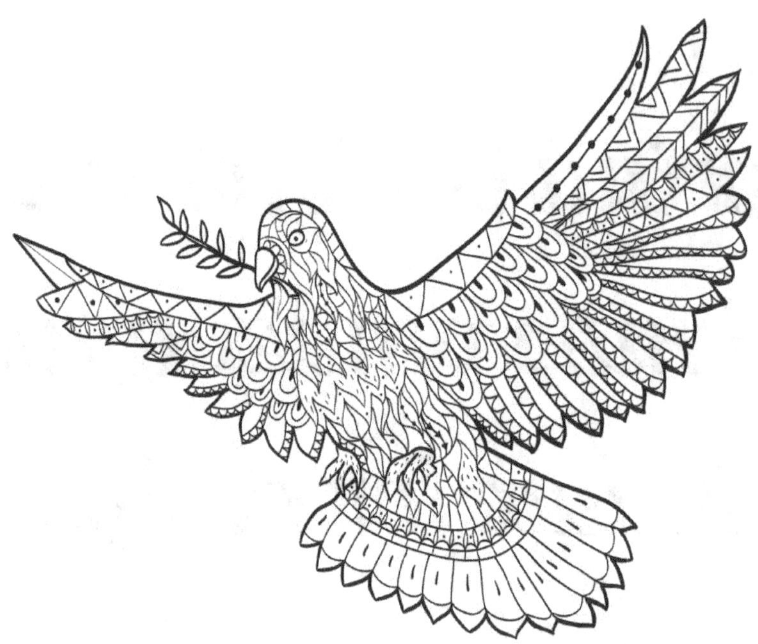

This coloring book is belongs to

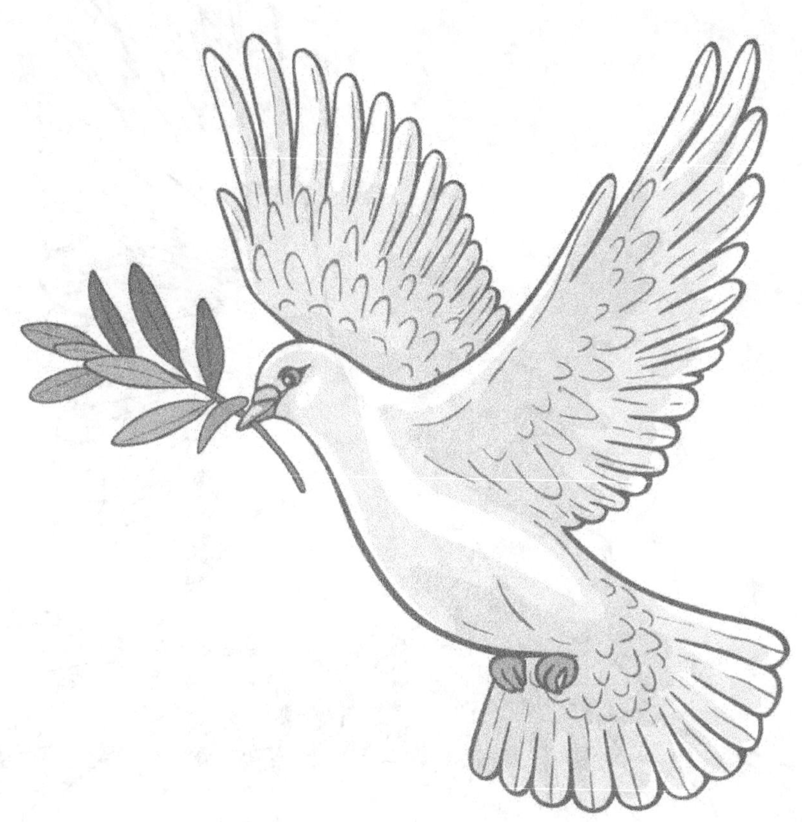

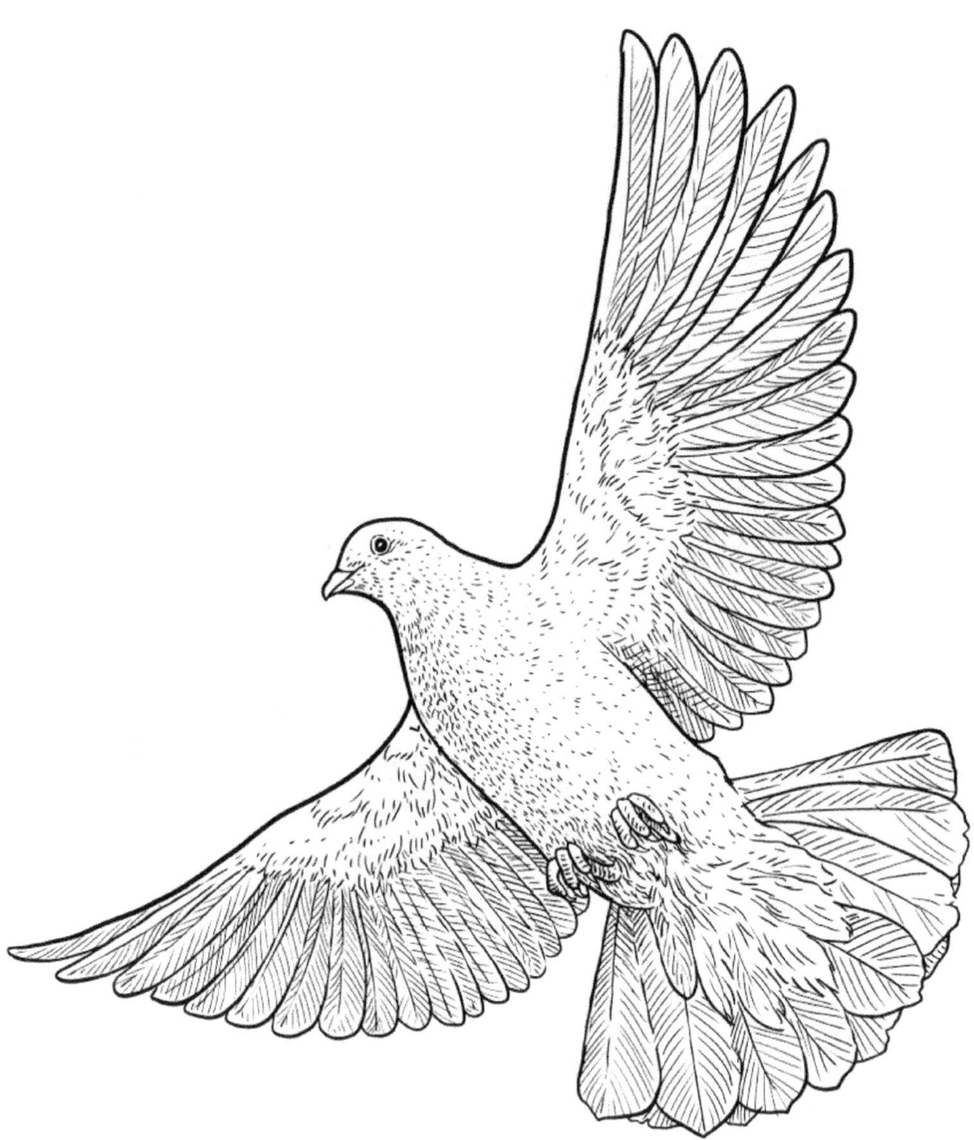

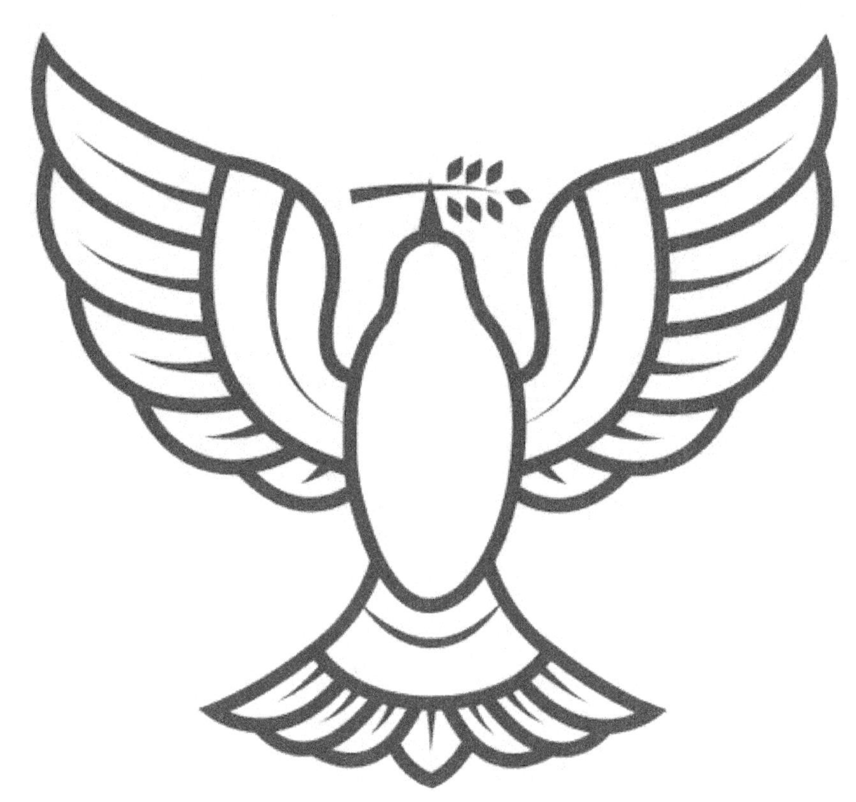

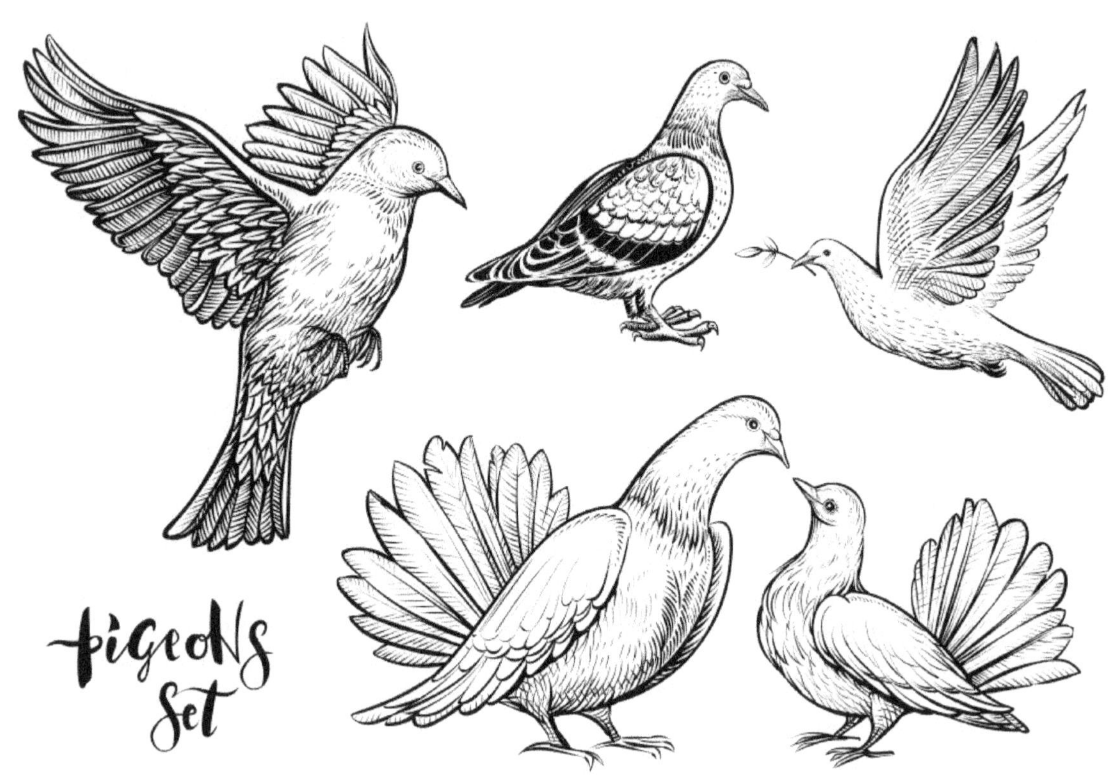
Pigeons
Set

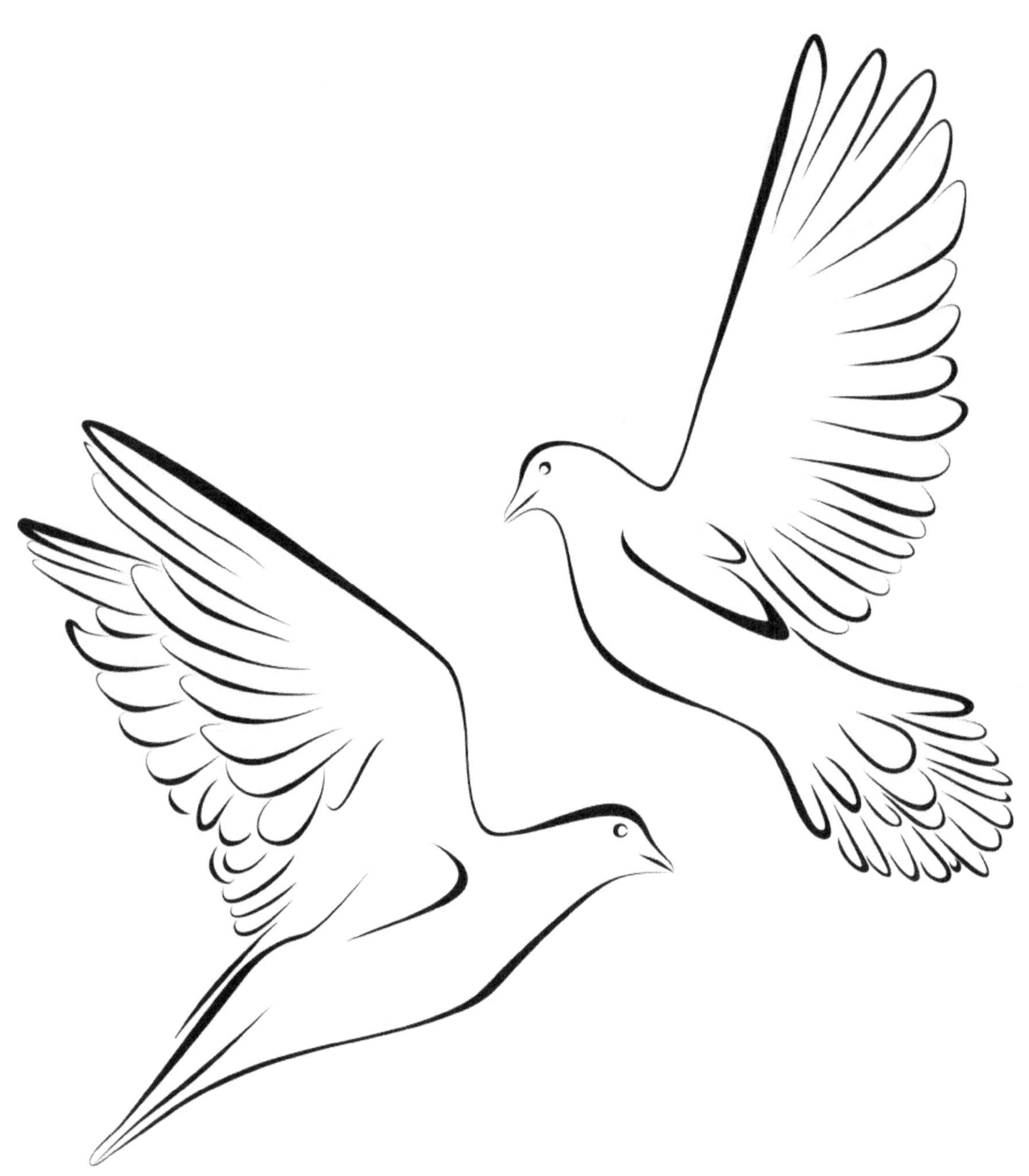

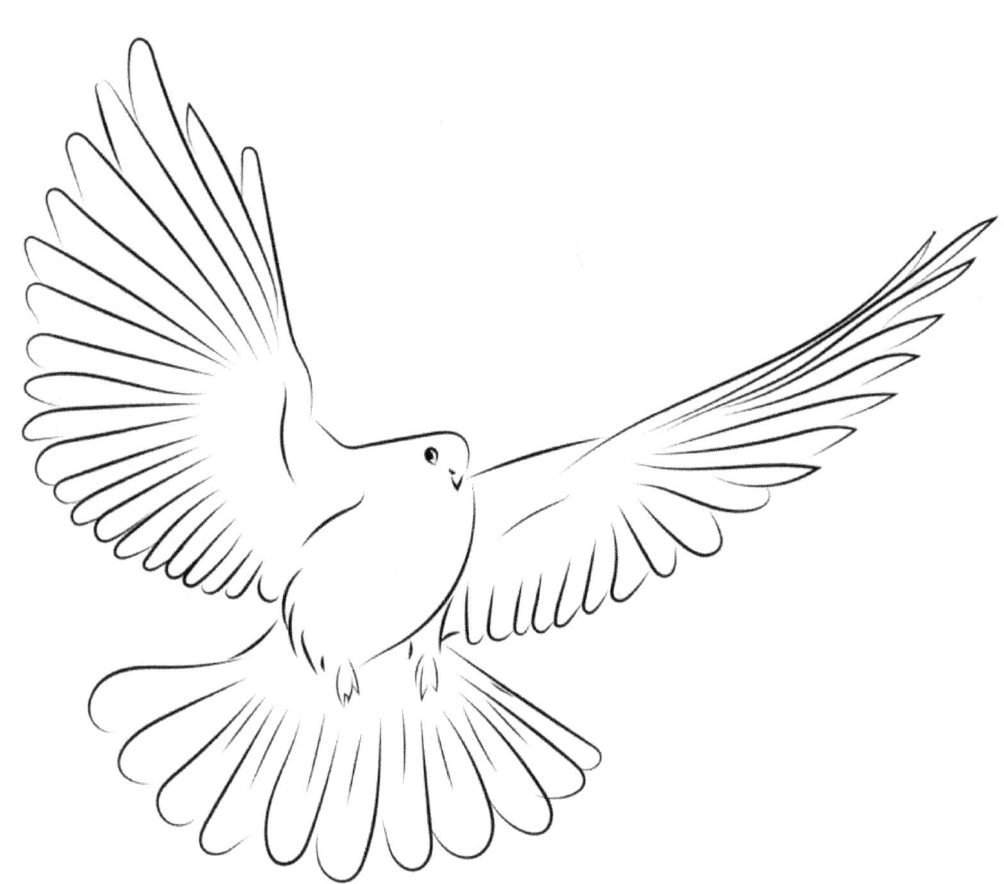

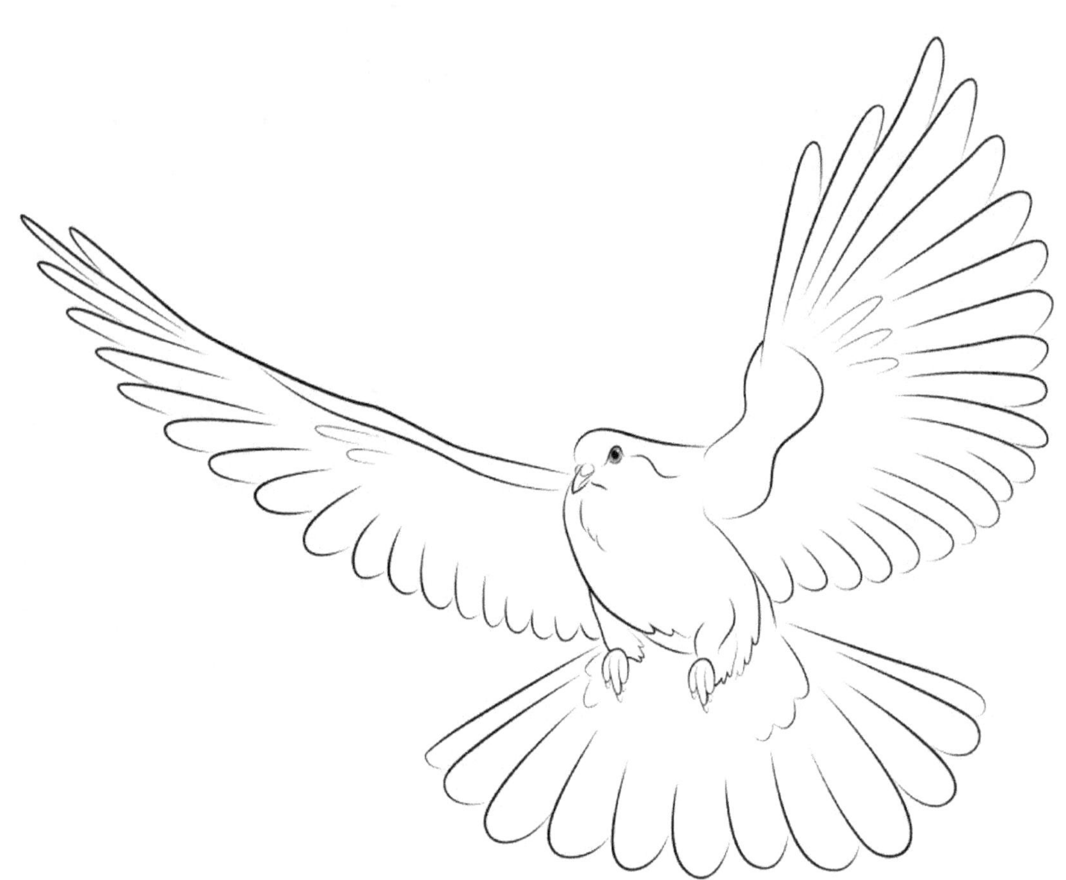

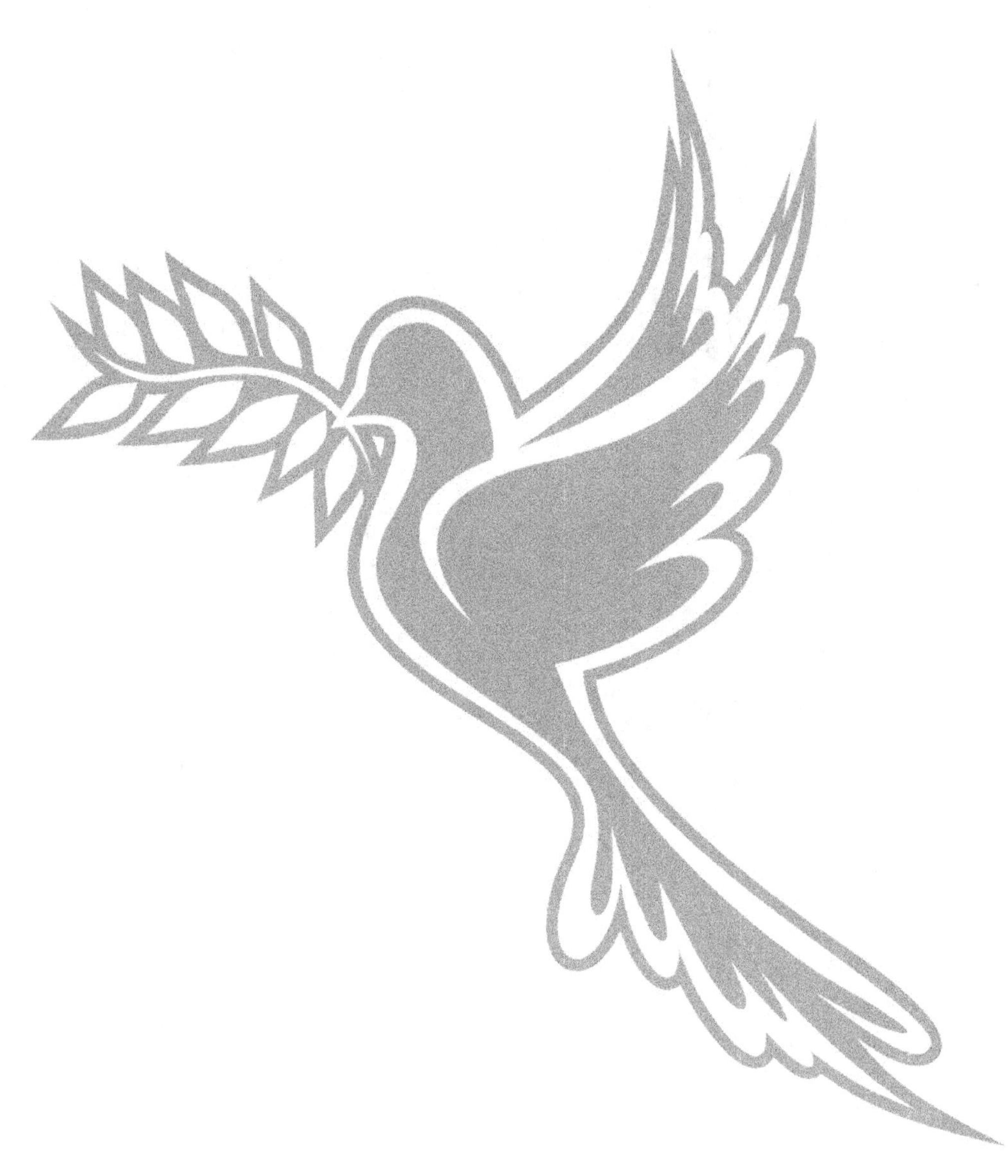

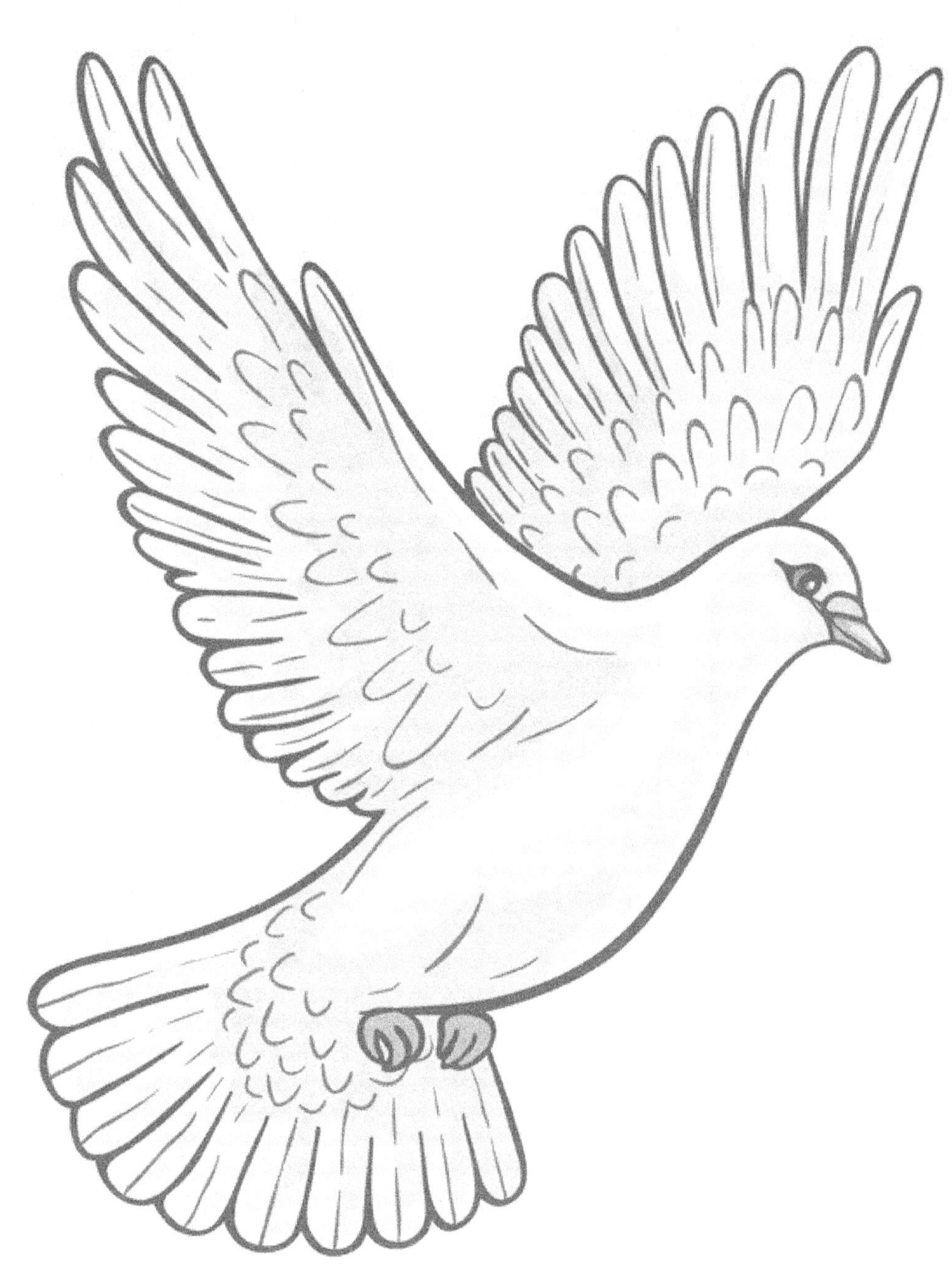

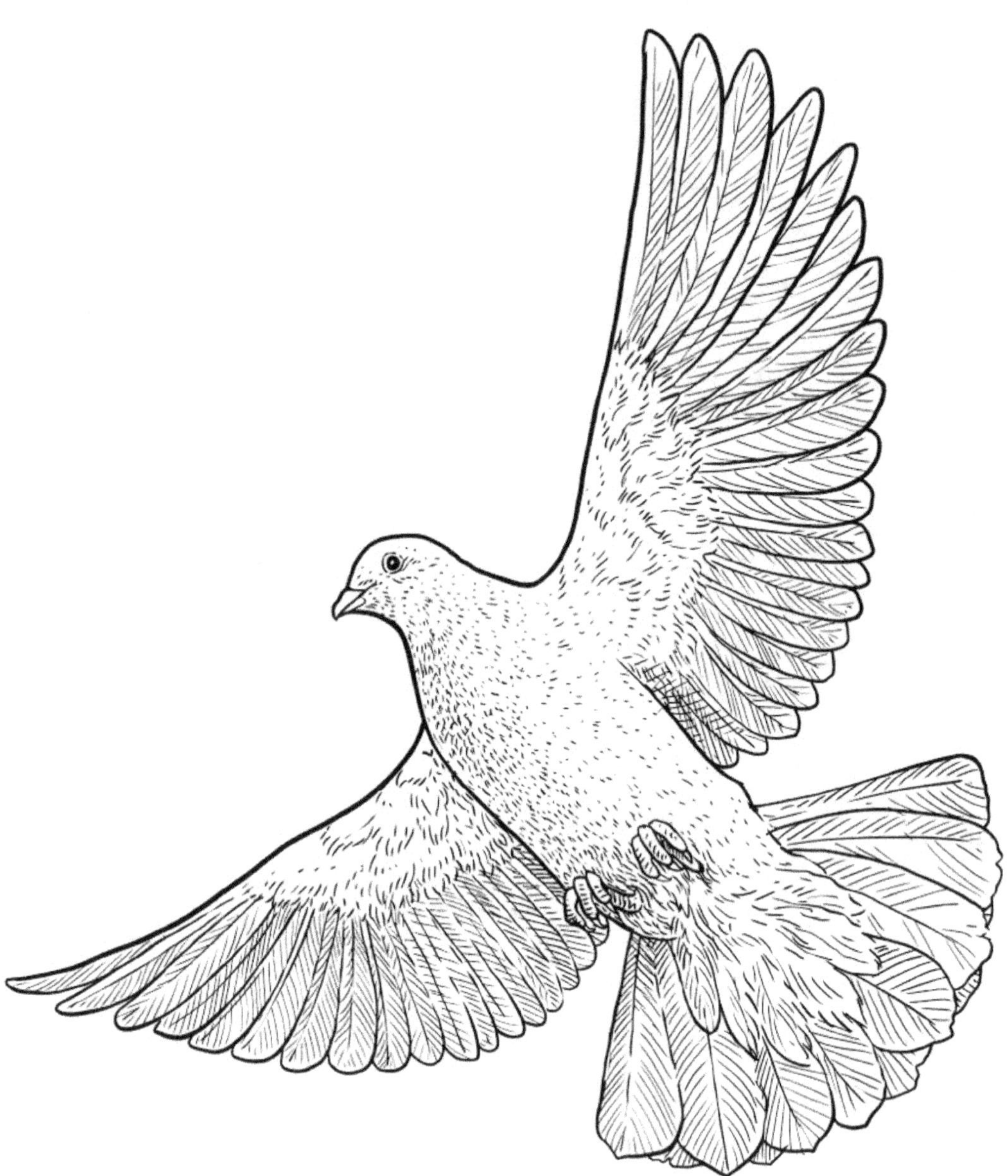

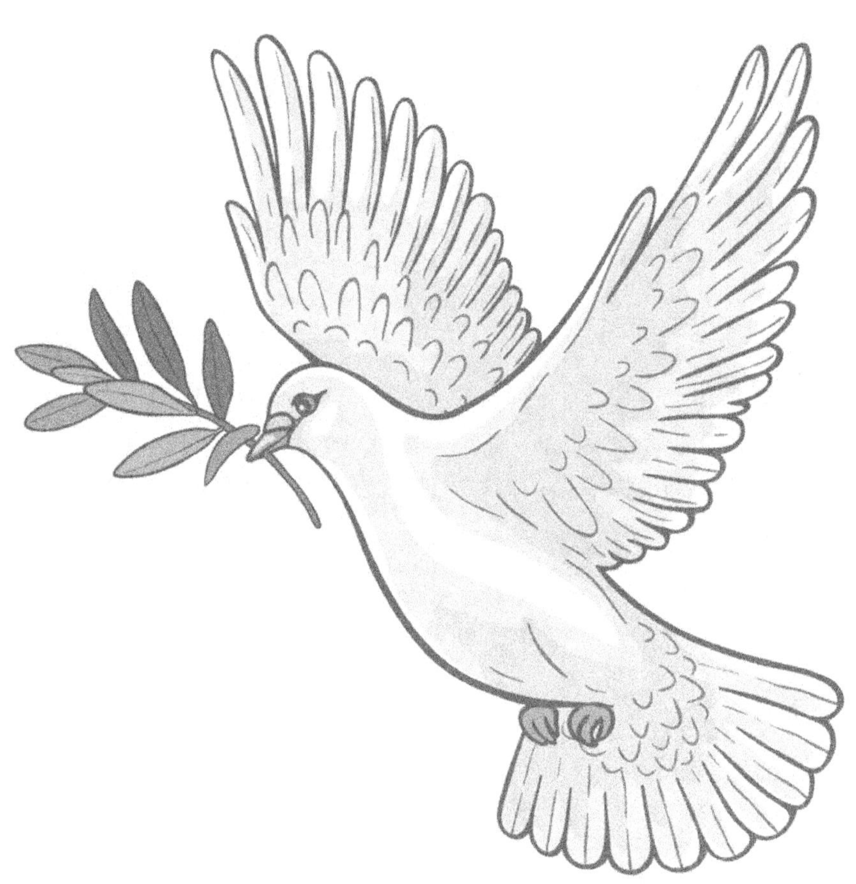

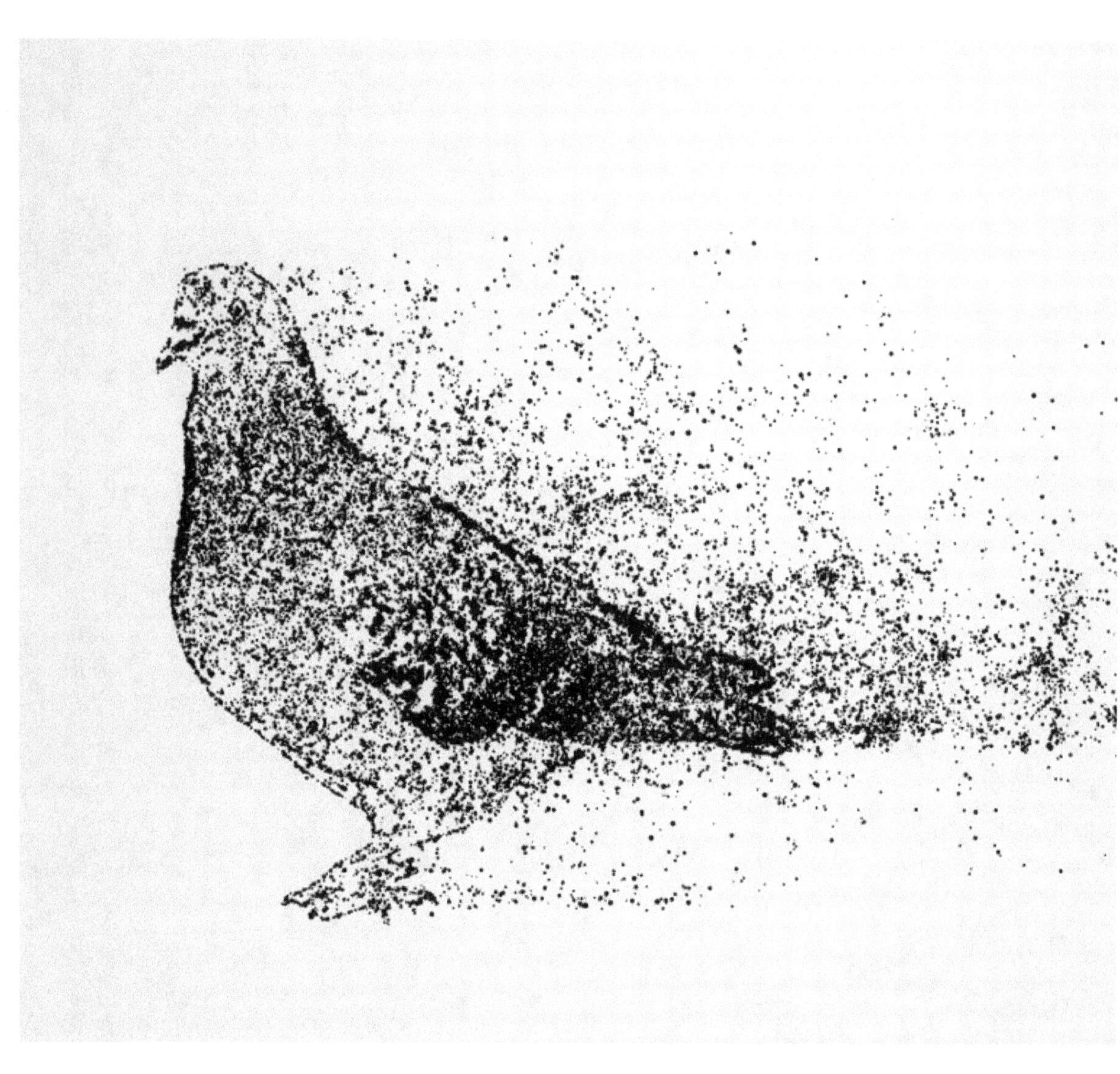

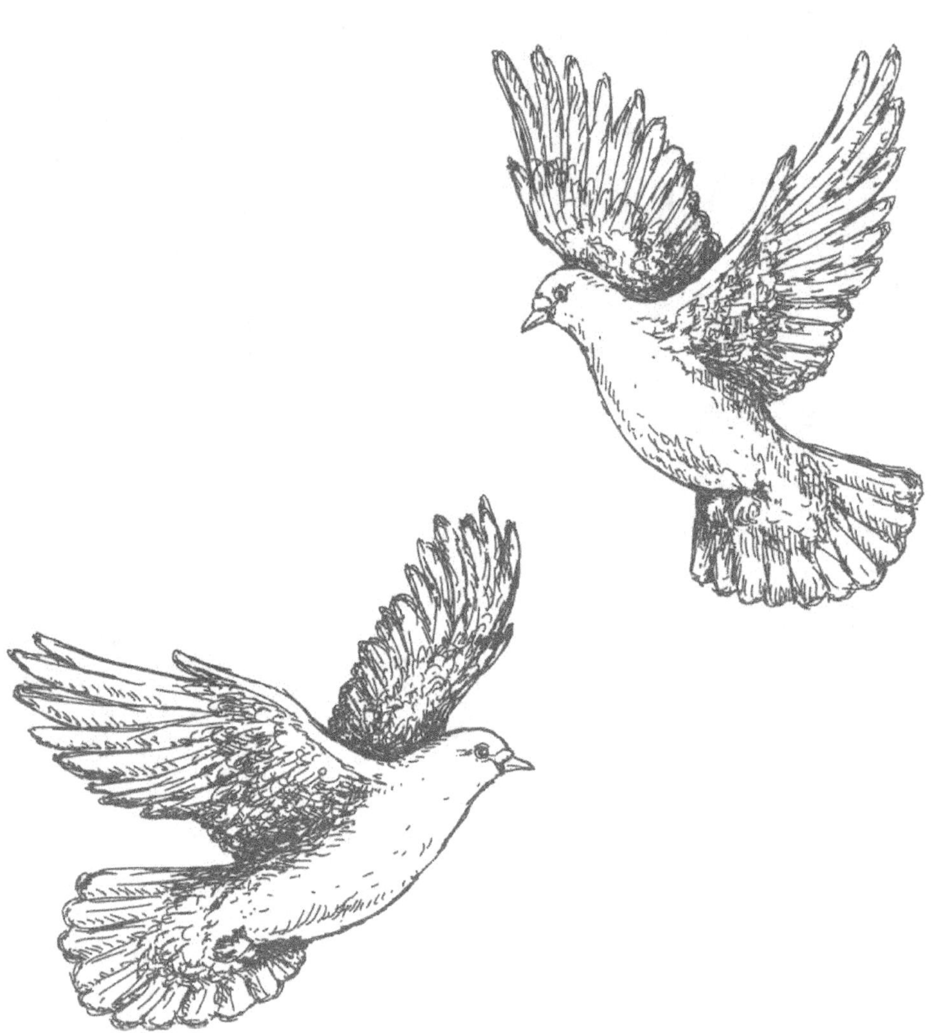

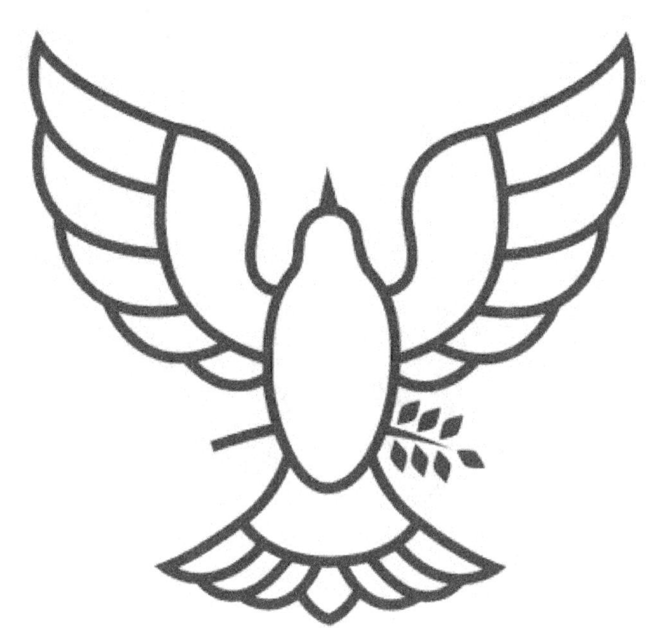

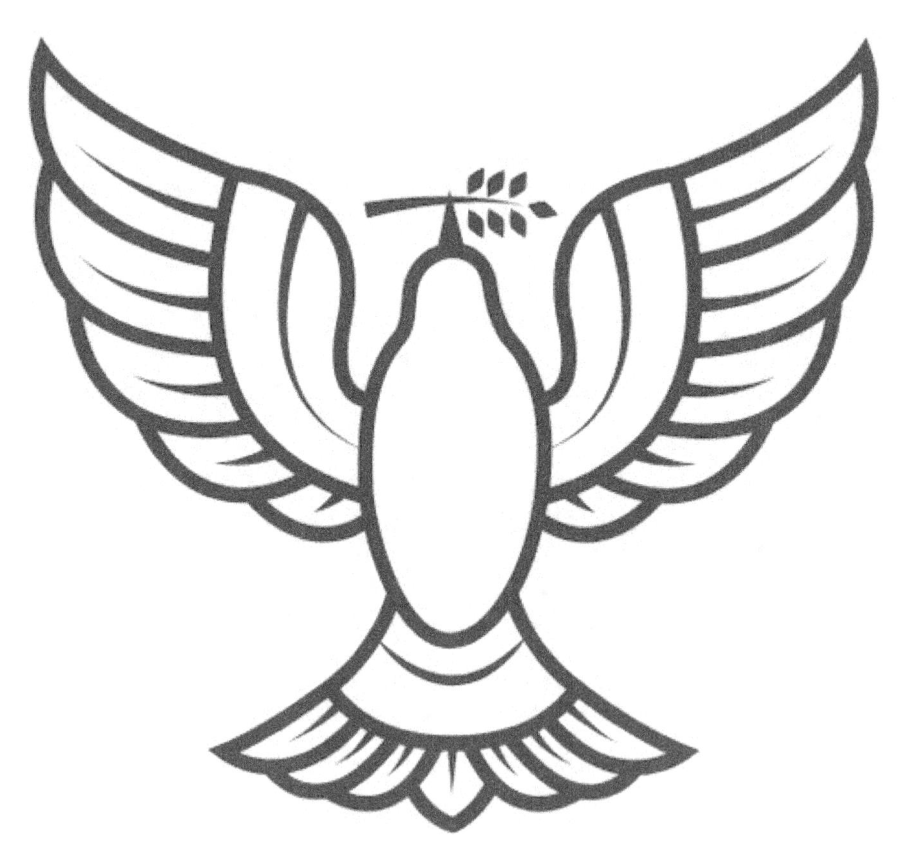

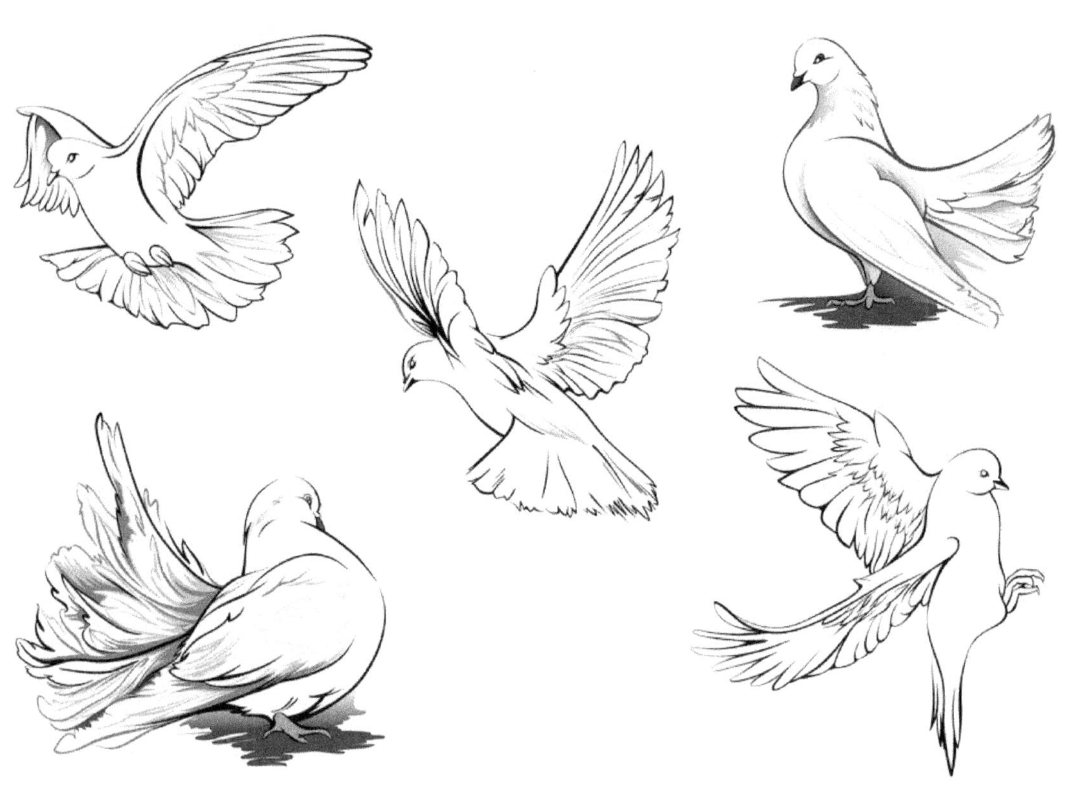

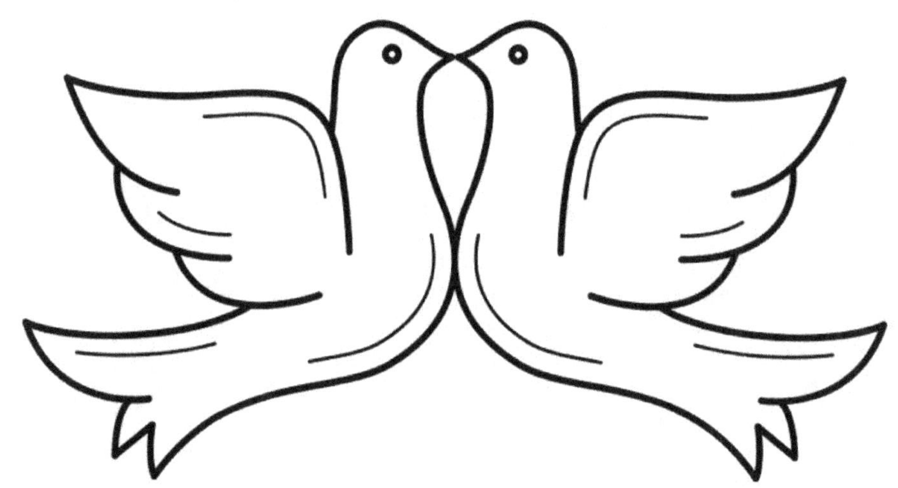

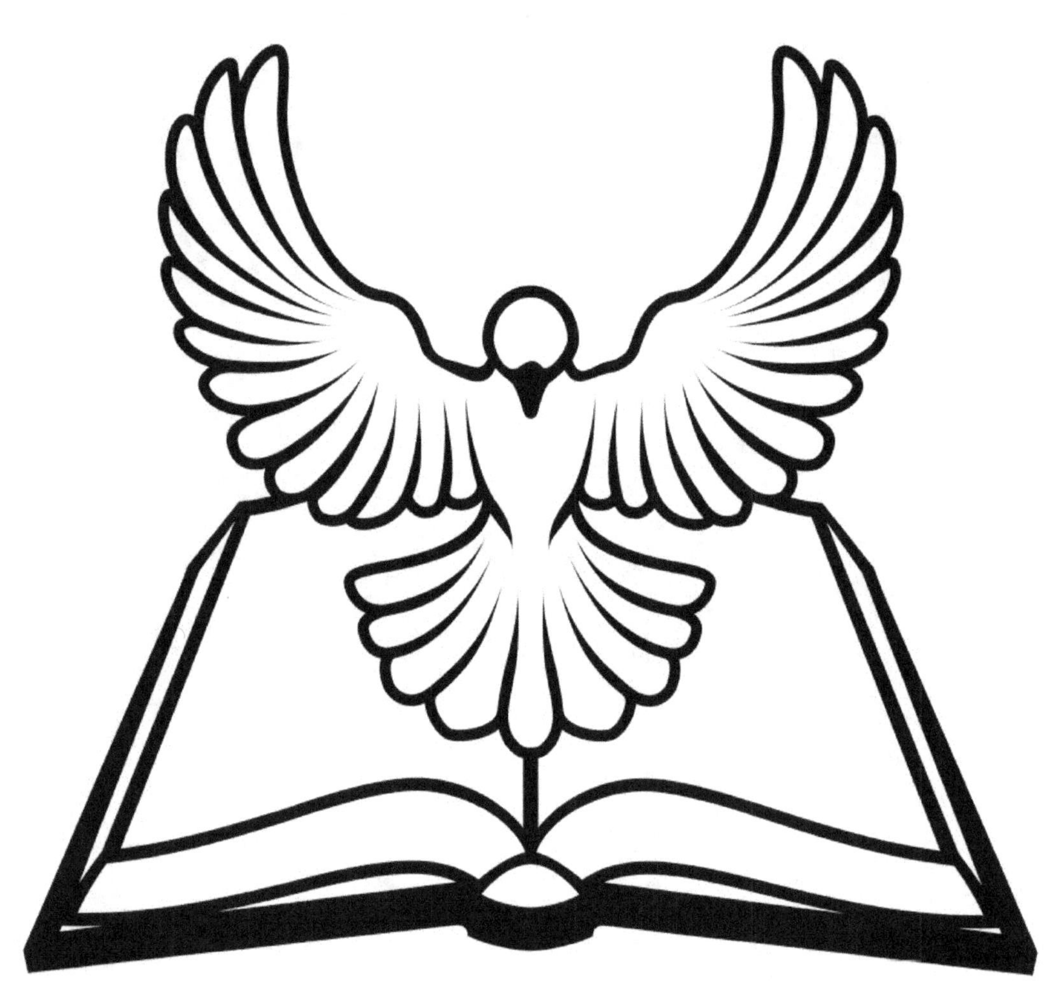

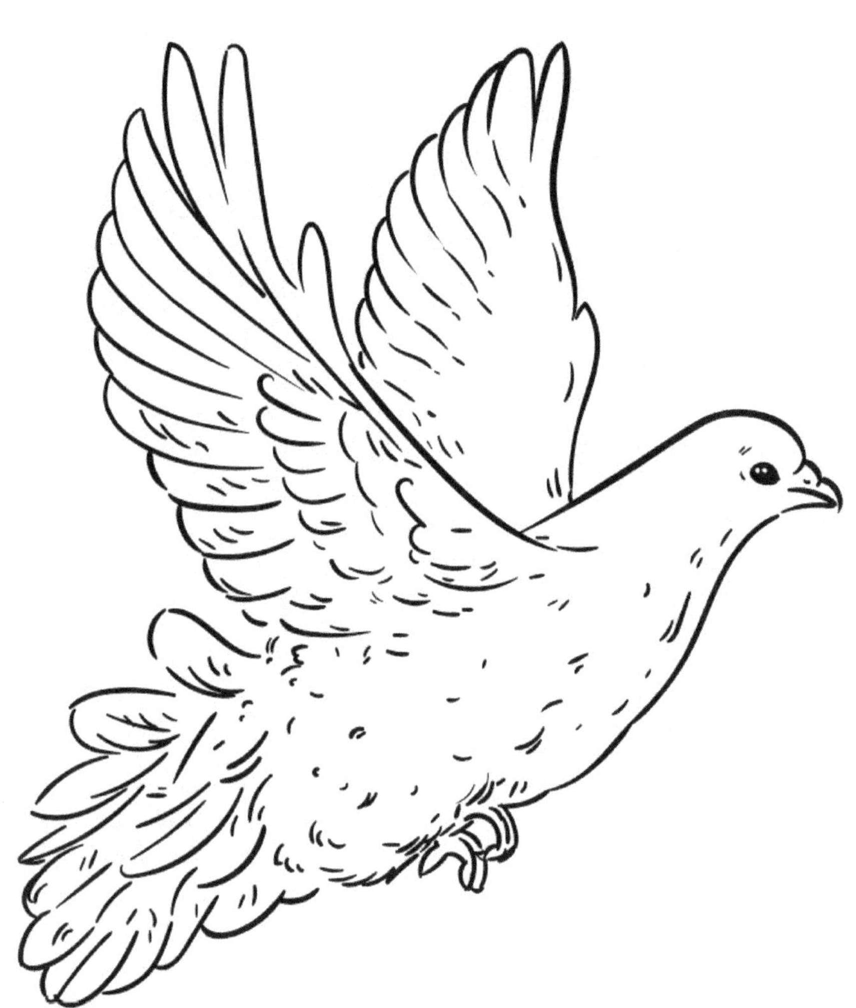

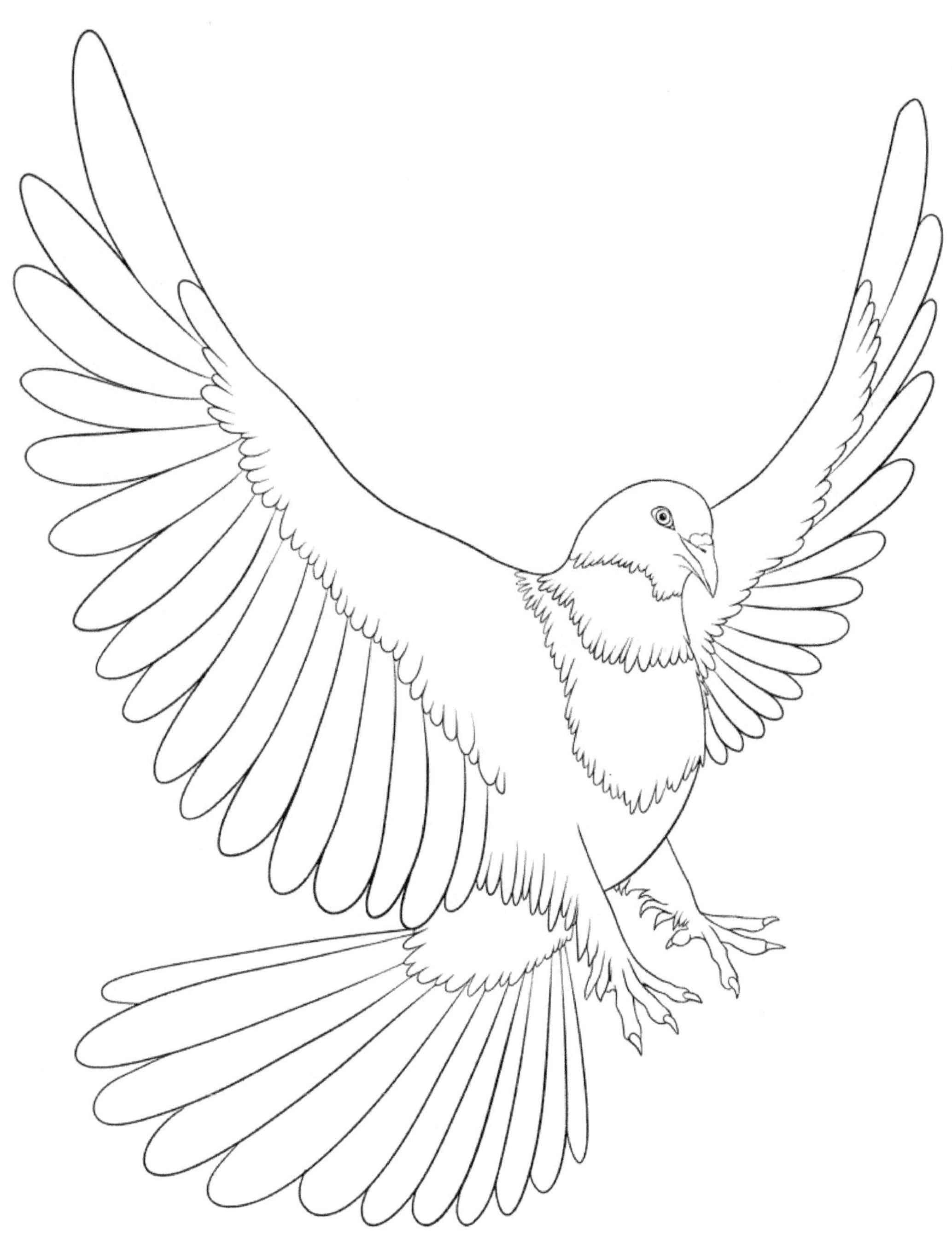

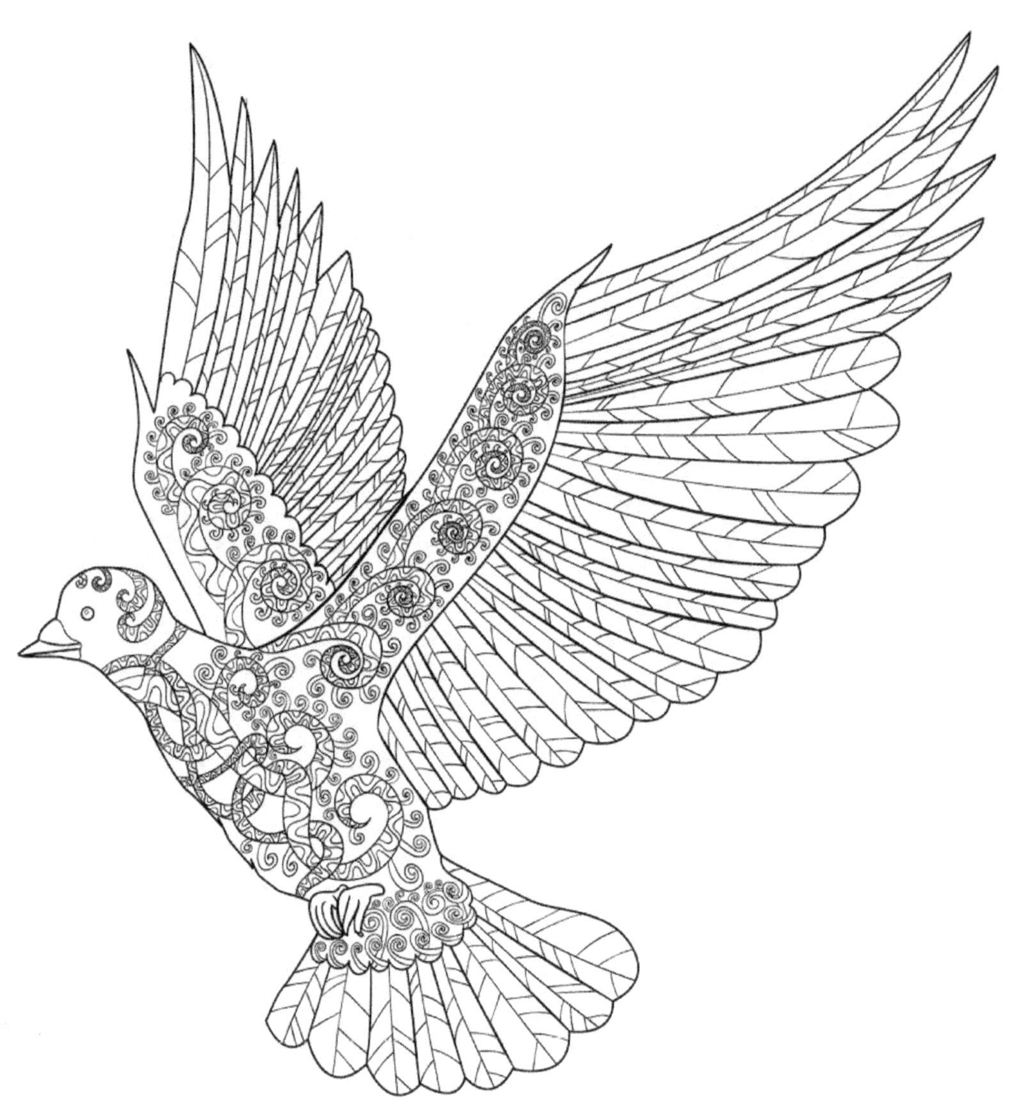

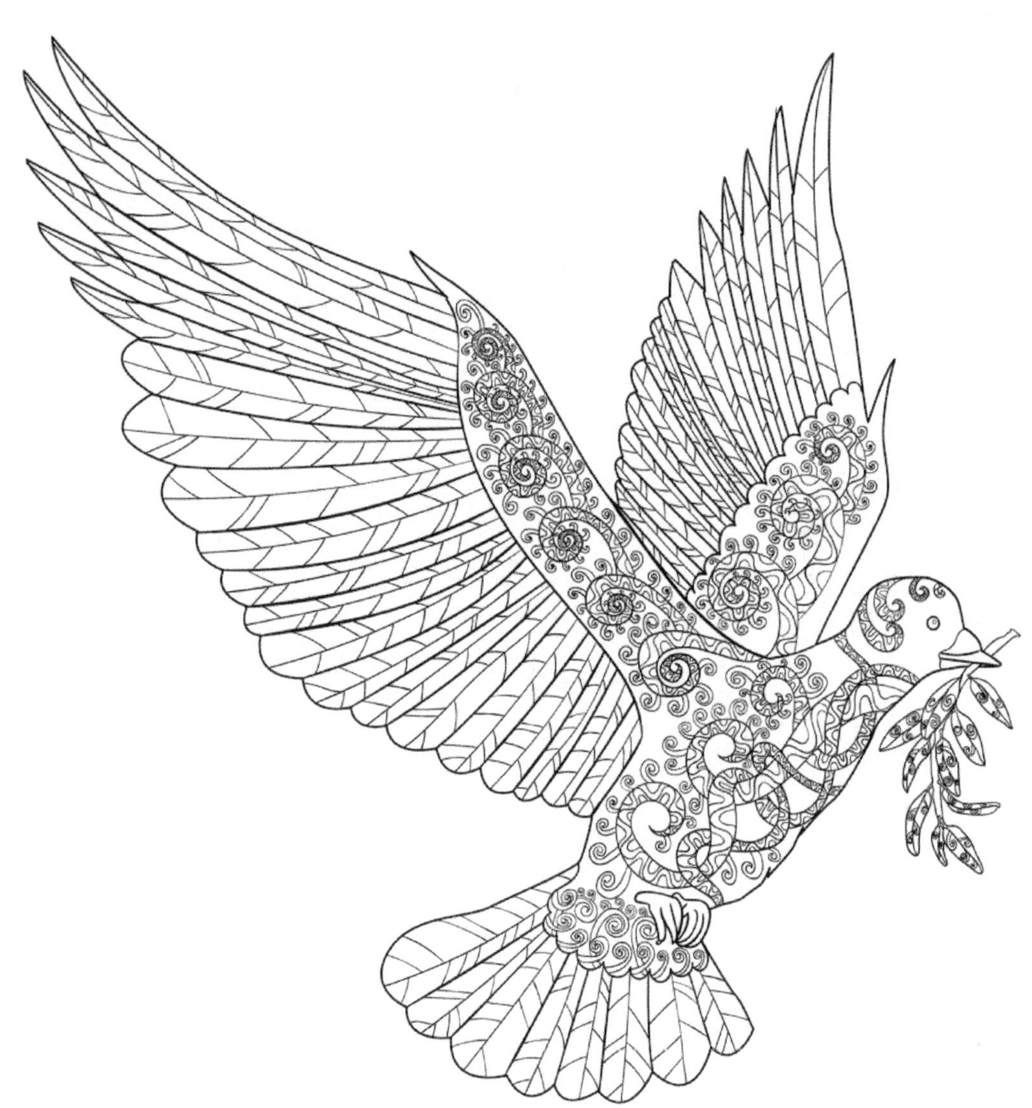

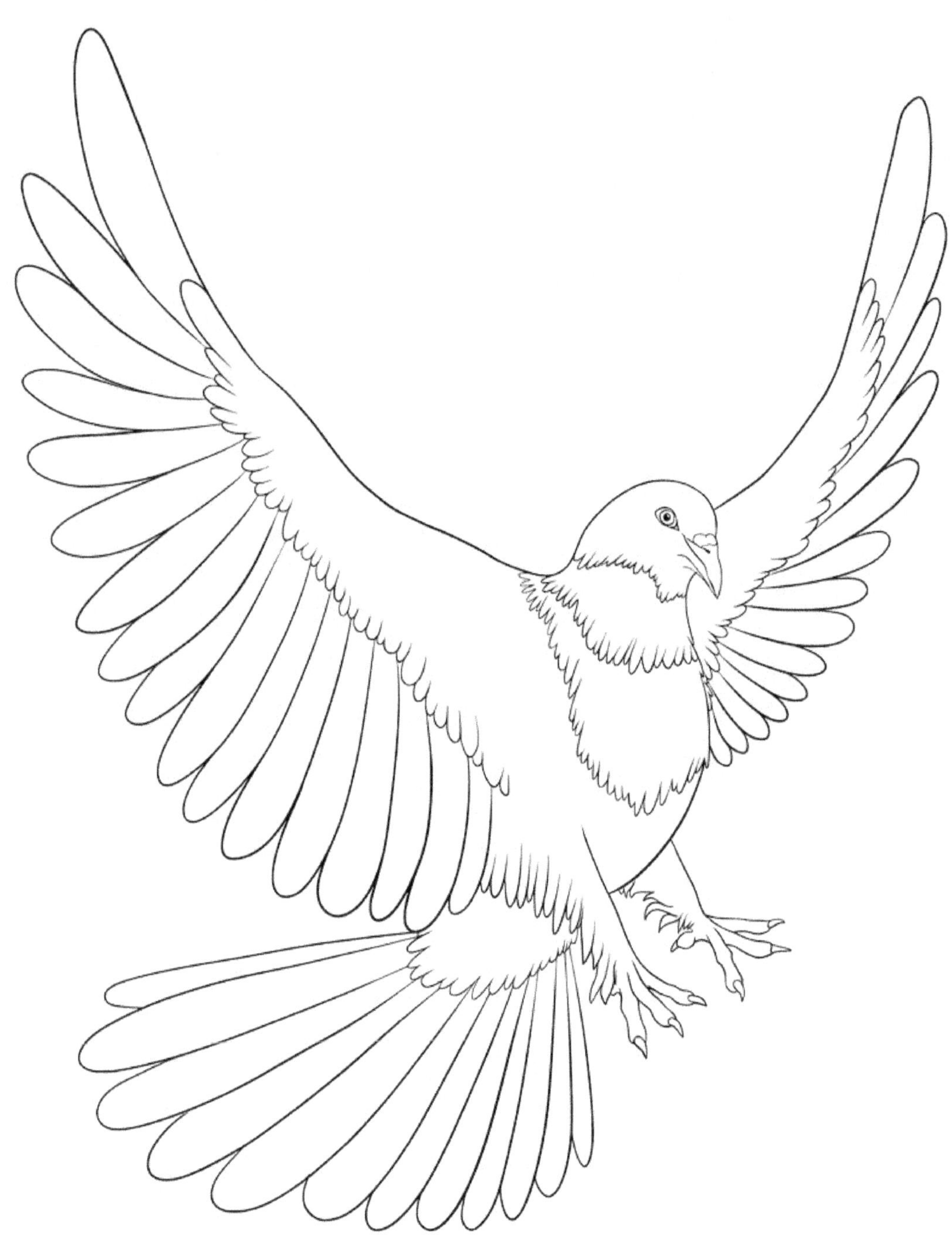

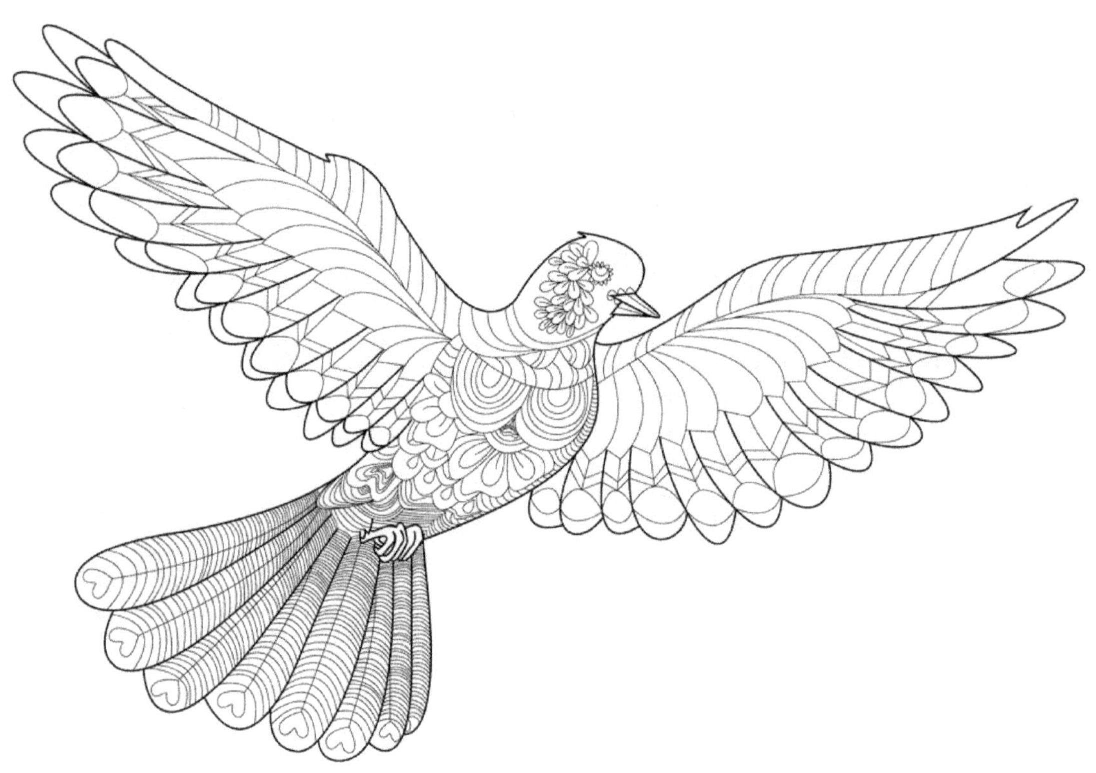

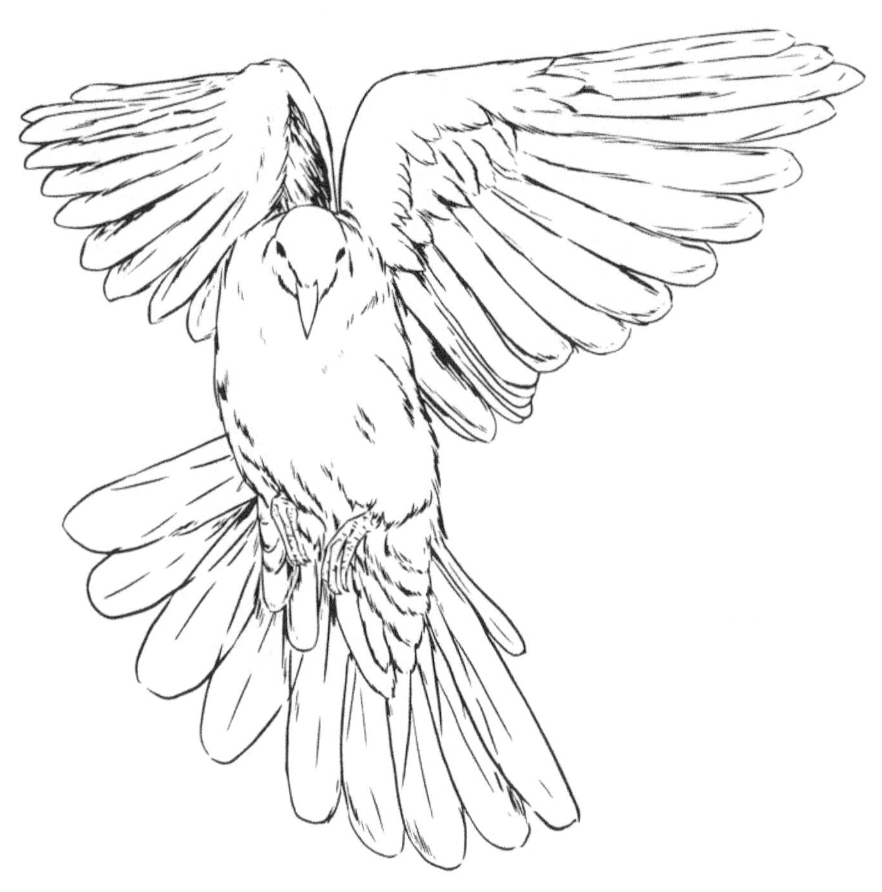

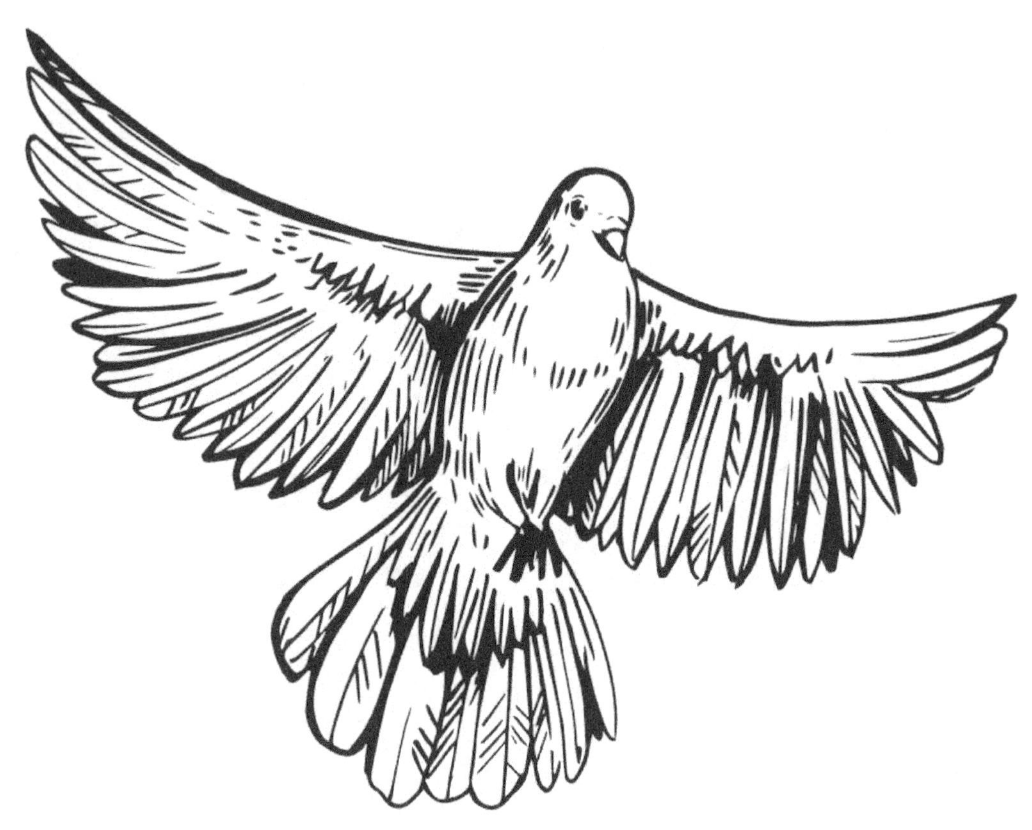

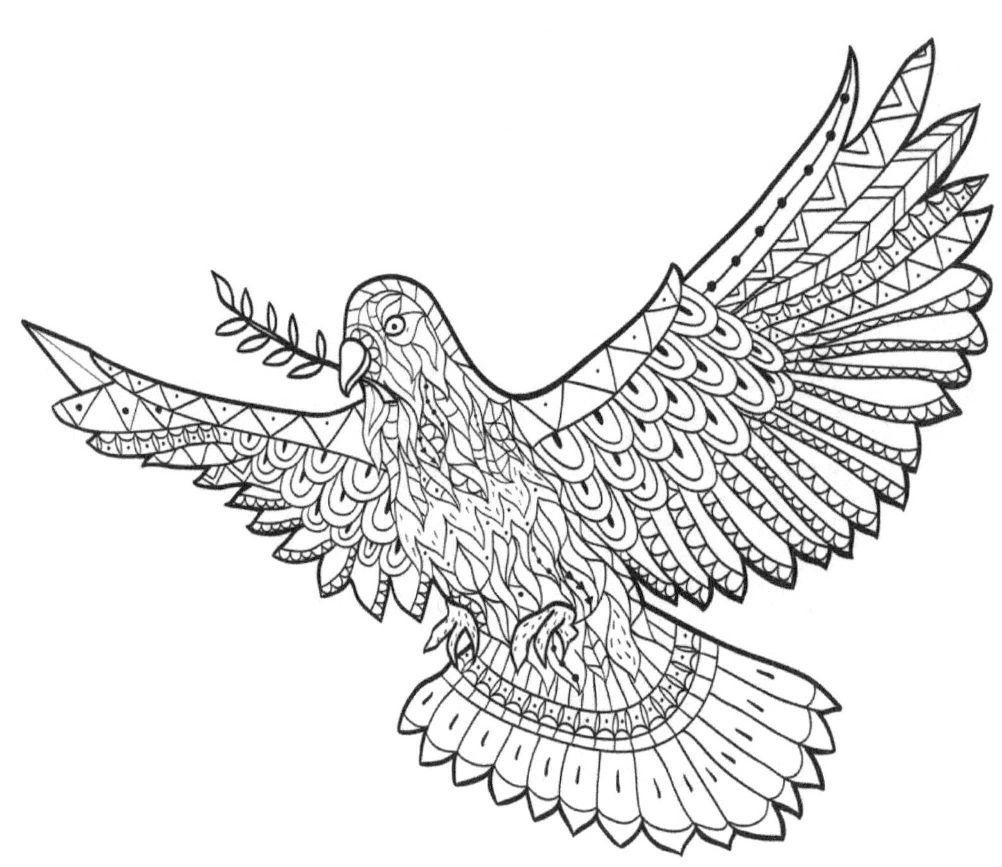

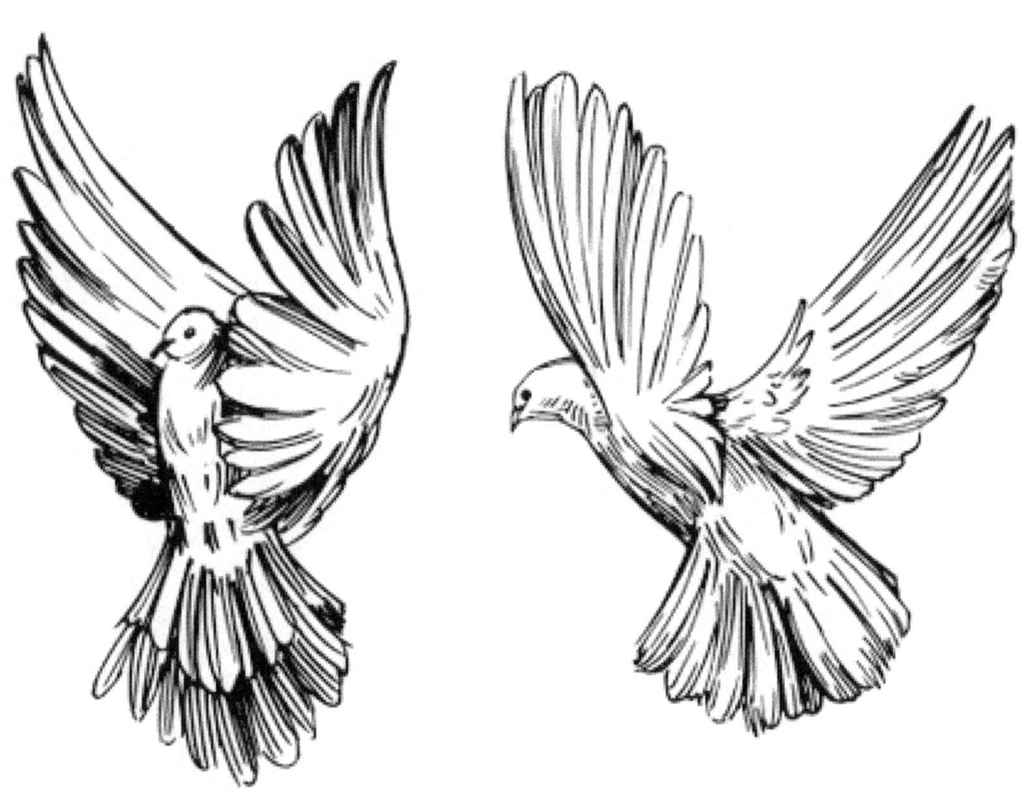

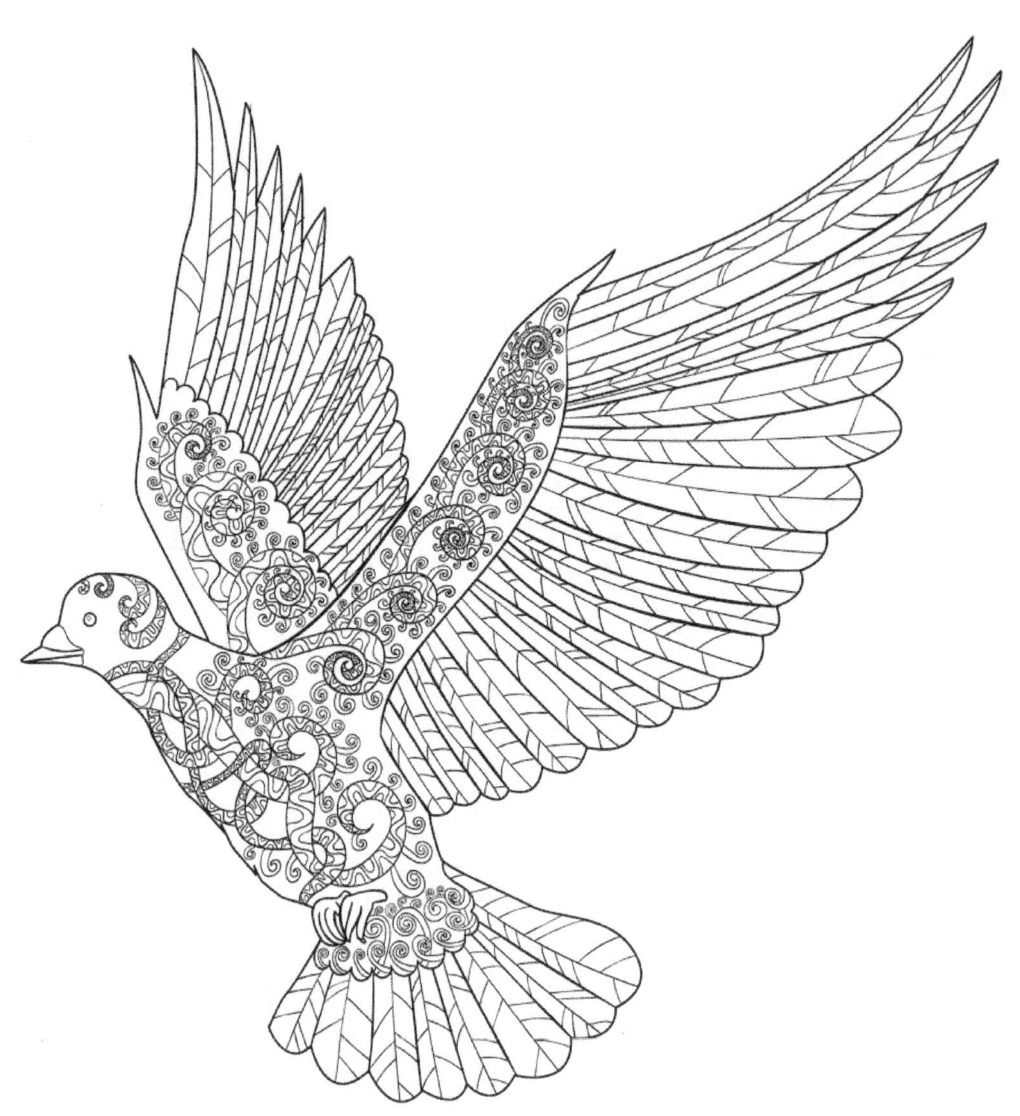

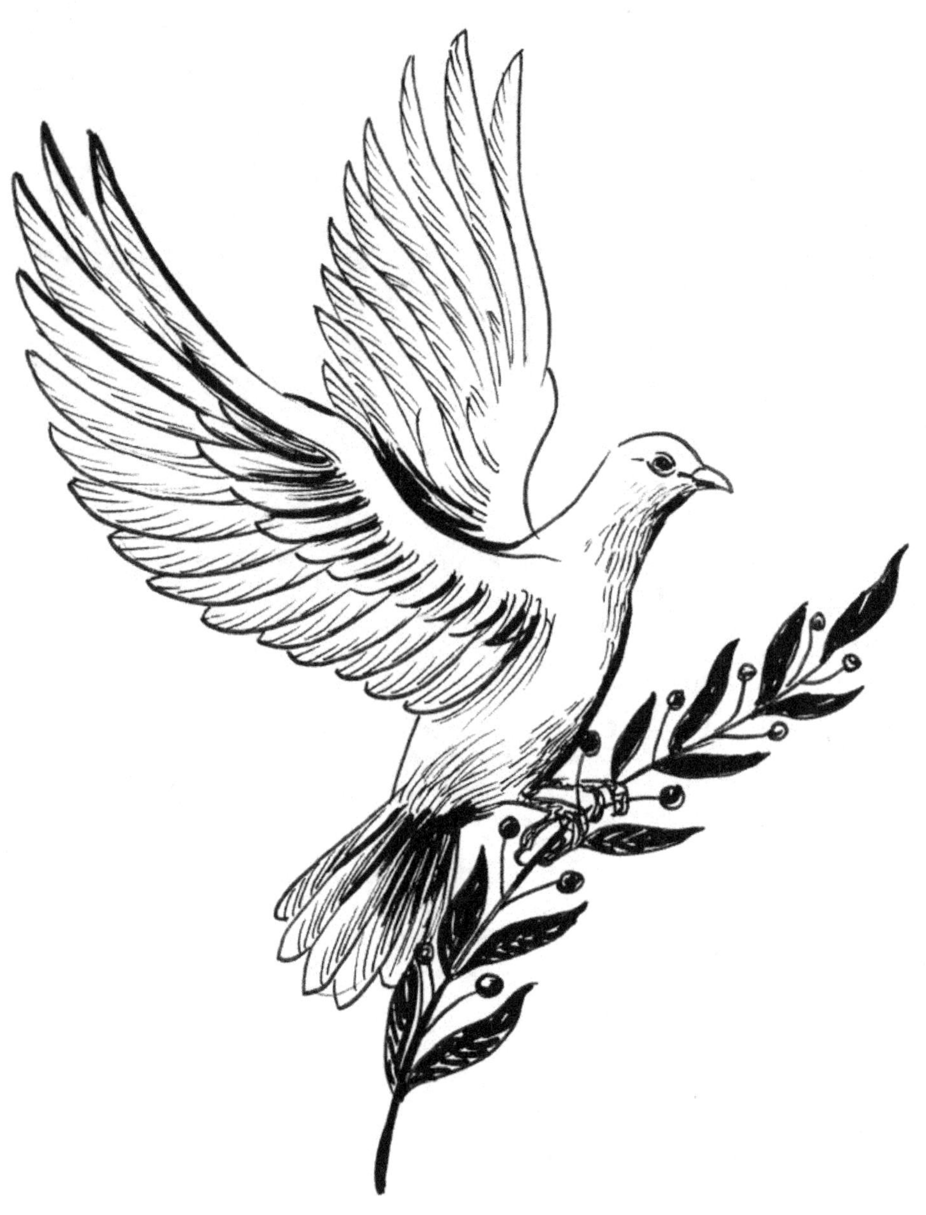

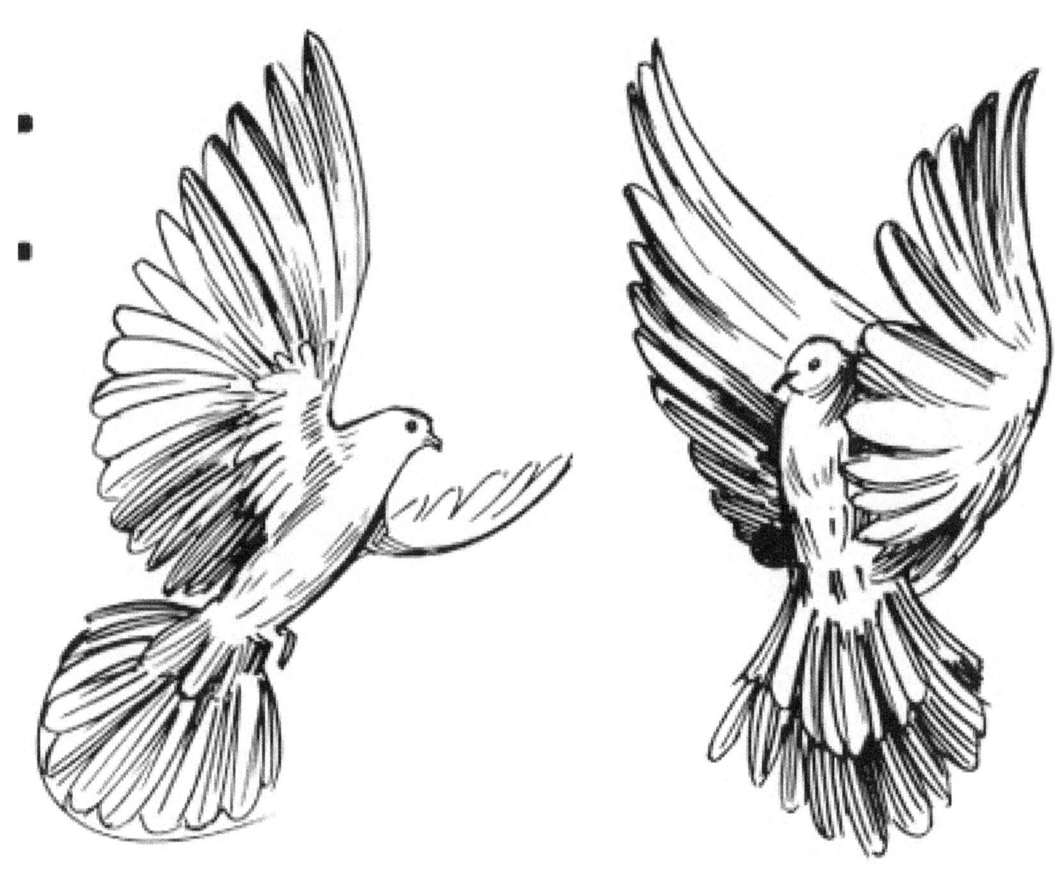

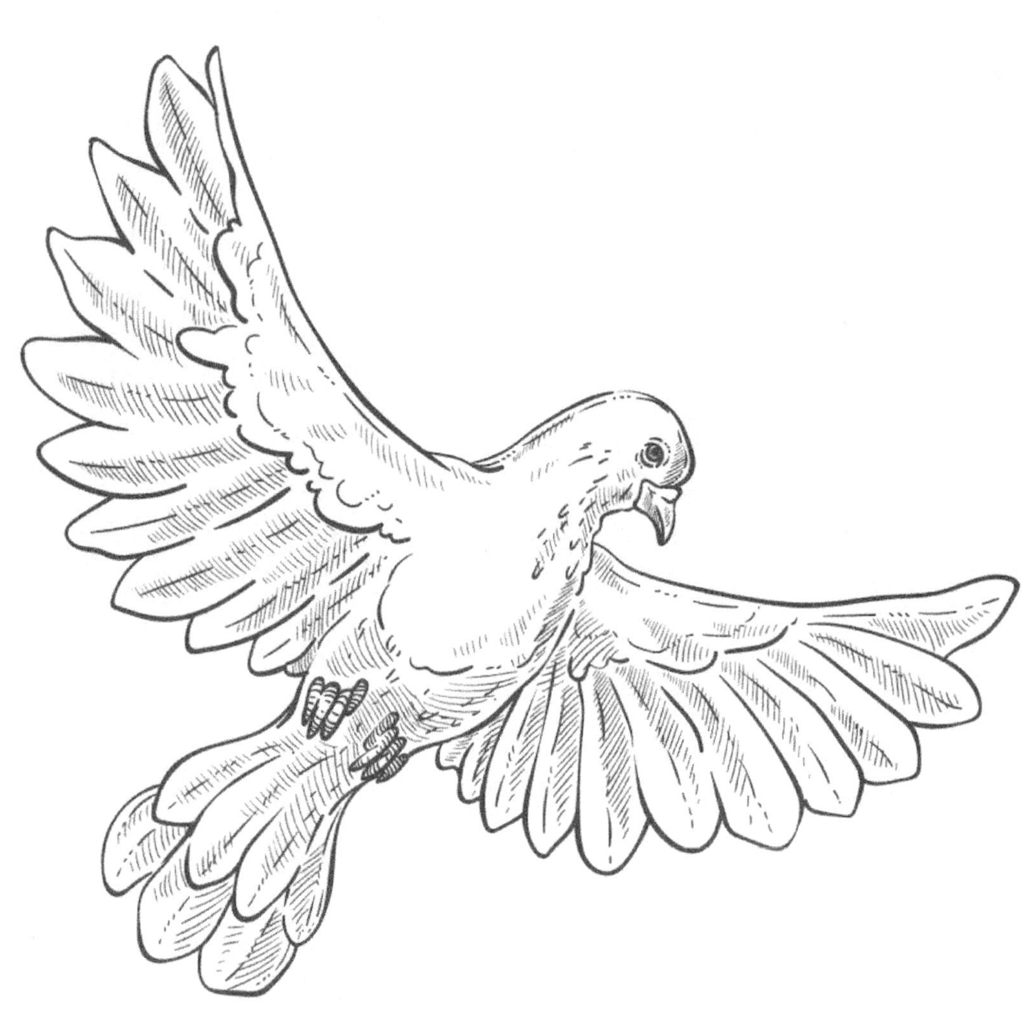

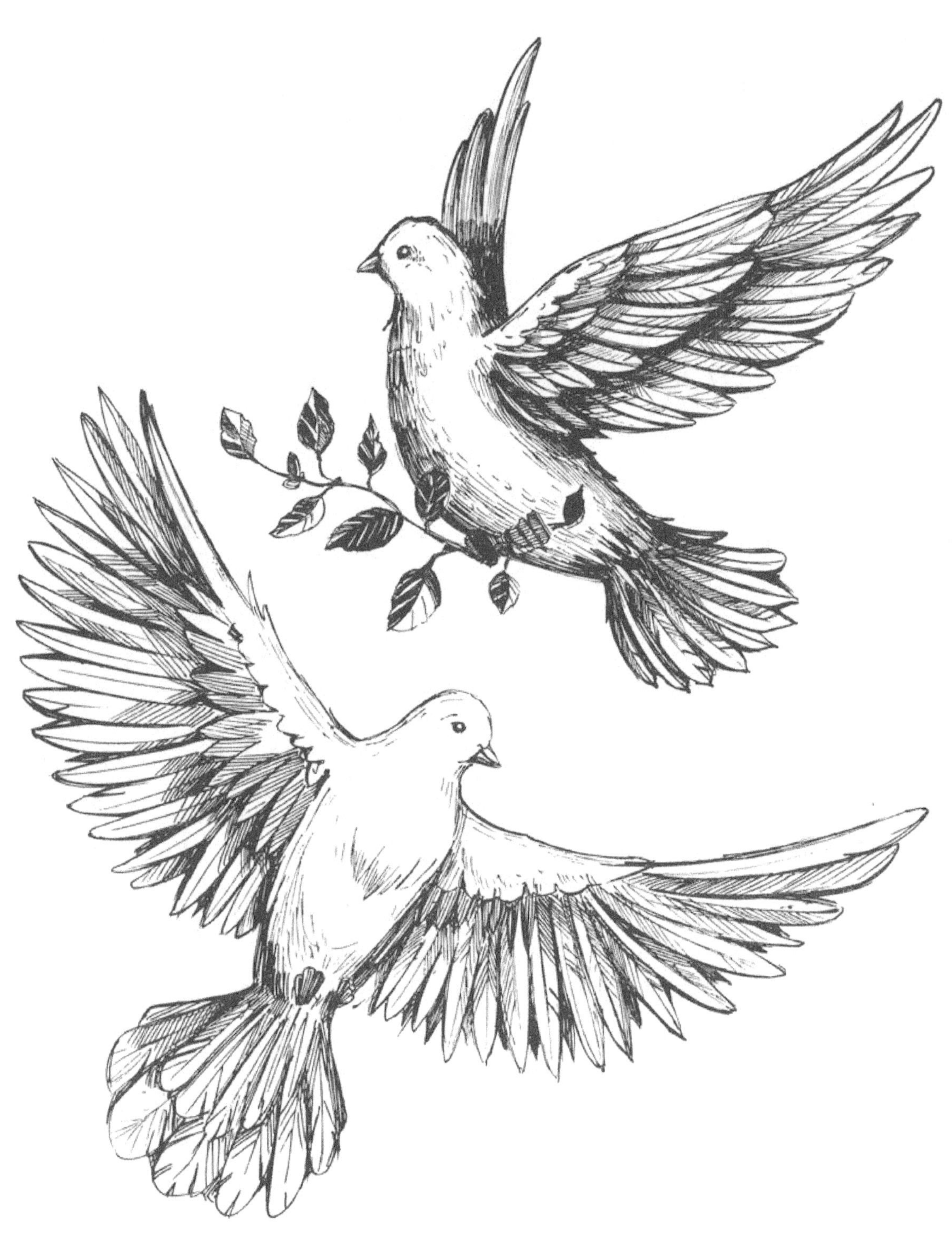

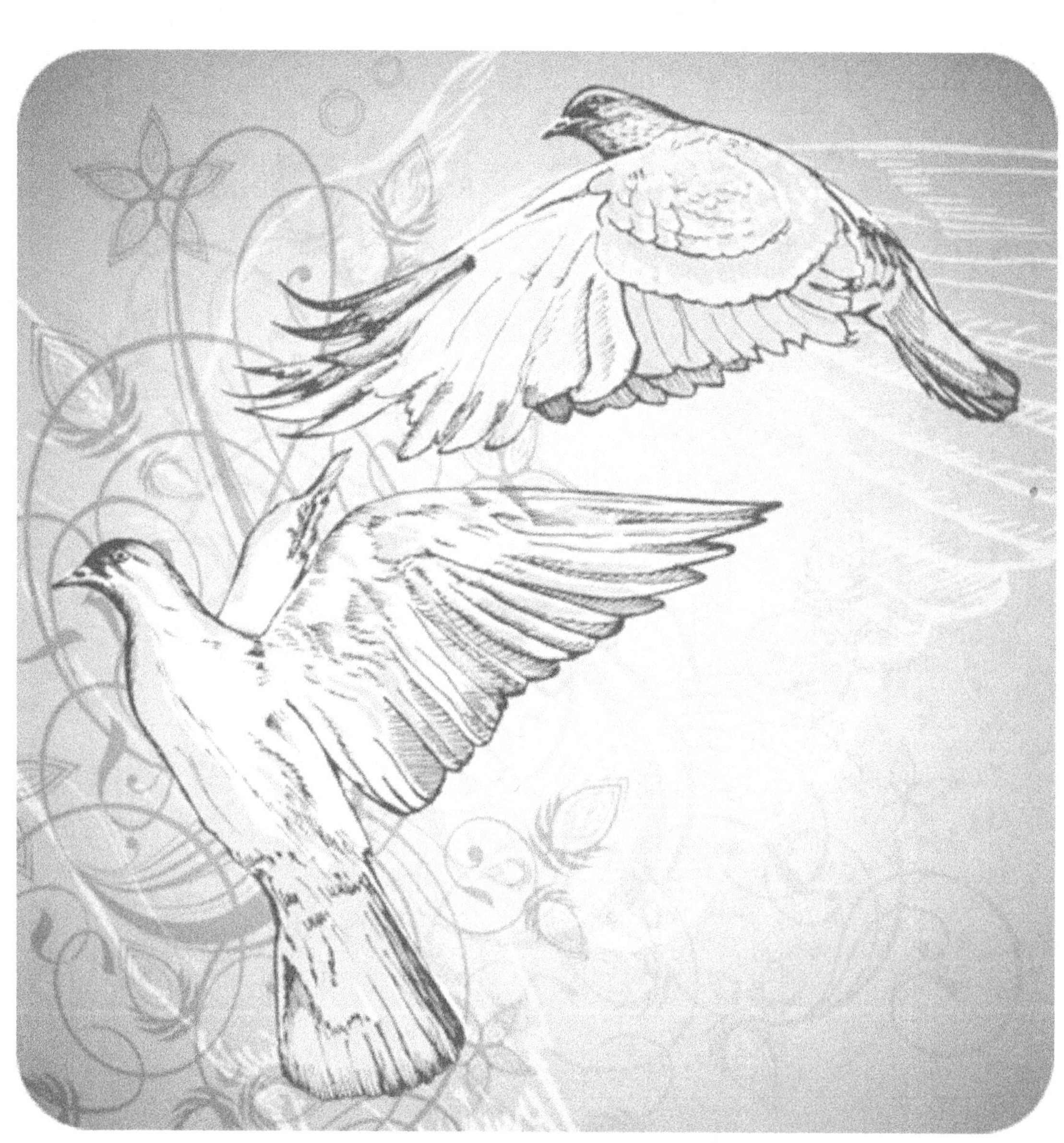